Forgotten Futures
a memoir

Bonnie Thurston

Cinnamon Press
:: small miracles from distinctive voices ::

Published by Cinnamon Press
www.cinnamonpress.com

The right of Bonnie Thurston to be identified as author of this work has been asserted by her in accordance with the Copyright, Designs and Patent Act, 1988.
© 2021, Bonnie Thurston

ISBN 978-1-78864-131-9

British Library Cataloguing in Publication Data. A CIP record for this book can be obtained from the British Library.

Designed and typeset in Bodoni by Cinnamon Press. Cover design by Adam Craig.

Cinnamon Press is represented by Inpress

Acknowledgements

The following poems have been previously appeared in *From Darkness to Eastering*, Wild Goose Publications, Glasgow, 2017 — 'Time Lapse' and 'Transformation'; *Spirituality* (Dublin) Vol 26 No 151 2020 & subsequently in *Summer (Liturgical resources for May, June and July)*, Ruth Burgess (ed) Wild Goose Publications, Glasgow, 2020 — 'Laundry Day'; *Christianity and Literature* Vol 33 No1 1983 — *'Prendre la Mer'*; *National Catholic Reporter Vol 41 No 17 2005* — 'Mourning'; *Passager* Vol. 50 2012 — 'That Fierce Space'; *Roundyhouse* Vol 42 2014 — 'Fire into Life' & *The Merton Journal*, 17/1, 2010 —'The Eye of Despair'.

Author Biography

Bonnie Thurston resigned a Chair and Professorship in New Testament to live quietly in her home state of West Virginia. Author or editor of 23 theological books, she contributes to scholarly and popular periodicals. An internationally known Thomas Merton Scholar, her doctoral dissertation was one of the first on Merton. She began writing poetry as a child, published her first poems in college, and is now widely published and has won and placed in poetry competitions in the U.S.A. and U.K. Of her six collections of poetry the following are the most recent: *Belonging to Borders* (Liturgical Press, 2011); *A Place to Pay Attention* (Cinnamon Press, 2014) *Practicing Silence: New and Selected Verses* (Paraclete Press, 2014), and *From Darkness to Eastering* (Wild Goose Press, 2017) A lover of the West Virginia hills, Bonnie is an avid reader, gardener, cook, and classical music lover.

Contents

How do I get to the Harbour? I called.
Two girls smiled at each other, pointed
the way I had come.

'Landmark' in *Above the Forests*, Ruth Bidgood

For Ruth Bidgood,
and Anne Cluysenaar
beloved friends, mentors, poets

...the dead may come to us still
or we cross over to them through depths of being
which words help us find...

'January 8' in *Touching Distances: Dairy Poems*,
Anne Cluysenaar

Forgotten Futures

Time Lapse

'The past is never dead. It's not even the past.'

William Faulkner

Sometimes in autumn
when dying is so lovely,
or in succulent spring
when life returns
with wild abandon
and speaks one's name
causing breath to catch
between chest and throat,
one has a fleeting sense
of standing fragile
on the very edge
of all humanity
might remember,
a sense of vertigo
as if all the past
might topple off
beyond the present,
and our so carefully
guarded secrets
flutter like falling leaves
into forgotten futures.

Betrothal

Winter's carnage is carried to a confluence
somewhere in the great downstream.
Ice is breaking up on the river.
Limbs reach crazily up out of the mud.
Starkly naked, peeled trees
are oblivious to hovering March.

A hundred snowy miles away
in another anonymous airport,
I drink coffee,
watch travelers watching me
in my European hat,
resolutely American face.

It is a time of dispersals.
The seasonal idiocy
of separation and return
acts itself out on many landscapes
making it seem foolish after all
to orchestrate these unions.

Home is where I've hung my hat.
Having carefully planted nothing,
a sudden springing of roots
frightens more than any snowy exile.
Accepting moorings, I am swept bareheaded
towards the river's mouth and out to sea.

Transformation

There is a crossing over
from which there is no return.
It can be chosen,
or you may find yourself
on the other side
not knowing how
your *transitus* occurred.

You may remain
in the same place,
dwell among the same people,
but all is forever changed.
What was can never be again.
What will be is shrouded
in a fog of unknowing.

Removed from the roots
that bound and fed you,
the soil has fallen away.
You cannot go back;
the earth has closed.
There is only empty air,
the waiting and the hope.

When Love Is Passed

When love is passed to you
on a bone china plate
like *Petits Fours* on a doily,
accept with gratitude.

Life holds enough
awful, heavy crockery,
and we have all eaten
more than our share of sand.

Advanced Technique

The first time
we made love
I ran my hand
down his long back,
over his buttocks,
down the sinewy
muscles of his leg.
I was stunned
by how hard
his body was.

He was my first
and only lover.
I was young and wrong.
He was fragile.
The most advanced
love-making technique
I learned was
to treat tenderly
the child
inside the man.

The Oracle Was Silent

You took me there
in pouring rain.
Delphi rose out of mist.
I was enchanted.

I inhaled no drugged smoke,
only the smell of your skin,
shaving soap, wet wool.

Being content with what was,
I made no predictions,
was knit again inexorably to you

by the spell of the place,
the gaze of the bronze charioteer,
the love that even death
cannot conquer.

Ought To Be

There ought to be poems
For ordinary days
When laundry is folded,
Letters answered, bills paid,
Beds weeded, flowers up,
All the essays marked---

Poems for days when storms
Are distant rumblings,
When the in-laws don't call
And expectedness reigns
Sovereign as the stars
Above a quiet kingdom.

Pastorals

I.

The mud in the river had just settled
after yesterday's violent rain.
We sat on the porch, silent and separate.
You tuned in baseball on the radio;
I absently read a dull book review.
A distant rumble bespoke our waiting.
Though wordless, we knew it would squall again.
When it began, you grabbed the canvas sheets,
while I scooped up the books and radio.
The rain ran down the fiberglass roof,
dripped on bushes not so thirsty as we.
You sat impassively while I made tea.
Nothing had to be said, for we both knew
this storm, like ours, would be blessedly brief.

II.

The evening fog comes up from the river
and settles cozily around the house.
Fireflies dance in the graveyard next door,
cast shadows on faintly glowing granite.
The grass you mowed in the heat of the day
lies down in orderly, parallel lines.
Soon bats (we know they live somewhere inside)
will begin the nightly acrobatics.
You smoke pensively, let your pipe go out,
and then send up a fresh set of signals.
Vaguely dissatisfied with slip covers
I made for our odd collection of chairs,
I cannot sit calmly while the river
is flowing by so nearly within reach.

Laundry Day

I am an ordinary woman
hanging out the washing
in a warm summer breeze.
However, like Jesus' mother,
I ponder in my heart,
today on the inevitable
imperfection of human love
which seems always to be
wounded and wounding.
Without evil intention
we harm and are harmed,
seeking in the other
what the other cannot give.
How ever many lights
one turns on in hope,
shrewd observers know
if nobody is in residence.
In arbitrary movement
of benevolent wind,
I use the last clothes peg,
pick up the empty basket,
head back to the house,
the commonplace locus
of my incompetent love.

Adage

An ancient maxim, older
than the Bible's fear
and fascination with its
defiling, sacralizing power:
'the life is in the blood.'

But it is not true.
When another month
blood comes as usual,
it signals no new life,
no quickening. Again.

Longing

Spring finally came.
The green, pastel fuzz
framed the branches,
power-puffed the bushes.

Memory boils with
the annual mess
of stringy rhubarb.
I stem strawberries.

The smell conjures up
my great aunt's kitchen,
Nana's love of pie.
In a red instant

I have cut myself
with sharp-edged longing
for the family
which never was.

Prendre La Mer

Tides set to separate moons,
out alone, in together.
Pulled along by their force,
we are pebbles at water's edge.

Outer and inner life
do not mingle. Currents and waves
collide at the still point
in the depths without other light.

Waters distort.
Murkiness, storms, seaweed—
ripples regular and unpredictable:
the off-balance produces life.

Waters clarify.
Limpid, pebbles on the bottom
seem within reach,
and moons float on the surface.

Nothing like Debussy's *La Mer,*
it is not the music of marriage
but its rhythms
which beckon to reefs and harbors.

The eye of the lighthouse
blinks, but never closes.
The tides come crashing in.
The pebbles and the water are one.

Beloved

Returning from a conference
half way across the world
that he, of another generation
and different expectations,
had allowed, indeed
encouraged me to attend,
a north Atlantic storm
made the plane long late,
led to spending a night
on an airport bench,
instructed by a bag lady
to use my purse as pillow.

It was a wretched crossing.
The exhausted crush of arrivals
poured out of immigration into
an anxiously awaiting crowd.
We were both tall. I saw him
before he saw me, saw him
searching strangers' faces,
saw his hungry longing.
Years into marriage I had
not until then known.
In the roiling confusion,
on foreign soil, I was home.

The Summer Before

It was a perfect late summer's day.
We had checked into the state park lodge.
Blind to what was around his corner,
he chose to take an afternoon nap.
But I was ripe for exploration.
The trail I chose was short and nearby,
a quarter mile loop below the lodge.
The path wound silent and fragrantly
through a needle-carpeted pine glade.
Turning a blind bend, I found myself
between a black bear and her three cubs
with nothing at all that I could do
but nothing at all, stand stock still, wait
for what, if anything, might come next.

The Promise of Lilacs

Delayed by winter flooding,
repeated late snows,
below zero nights,
finally lilacs bloom,
pale lavender, deep purple
scented sentinels of spring.
They are fragile, fleeting,
ephemeral as breath.
Image beloved of poets,
lilacs briefly signal life,
swiftly, silently perish.
Like them, my love,
I will not trouble you
when I depart.

After

We are a select sorority,
we who nursed the beloved
'till death did us part',
watched the man become child
to be fed, washed, changed,
watched him slip away
inch by awful inch.

Like a dervish on a still point,
everything revolved around him
and knowing he was going.
Then he was gone.
'I could have cared for him
forever,' we think, 'but not
live a day without him.'

But we do live on, and
the cavern caring leaves
when it finally ceases
yawns at life's center,
a tangible nothingness
in a turning world
ground to a hollow halt.

The Eye of Despair

Sometimes the best
you can do
is to howl.
When the wound
is so deep
you know the hurt
will never heal,
when the world
is so broken
a universe of prayer
won't repair it,
the best you
can do is howl.

Throw your head back
and (I dare you)
howl like a banshee,
like a she wolf,
like the wild thing
buried in your bones,
and feel rising
from deep, dark places
with the primal power
of your breath
a sliver of hope
to hurl with your howl
at the eye of despair.

How to Grieve

Stare it in the mangled face.
Do not turn away
or accept facile distraction.
Do not allow words
to be imposed on you,
platitudes of hope
dispensed like spiritual aspirin
by those who have not been here.

Do not deny your pain
or allow its trivialization.
You must grieve it
to the bitter bottom, the dregs,
the margins of life
where you will totter
at the edge of the void.
This is the only exorcism.

Suffering has no solution.
But, given time, far more
than the untouched imagine,
it can be moved through.
Others have.
You might.
Eventually blessing may
embrace the wound.

Mourning

The old folks call it
'wearing the willow.'
I think of a great,
green droop of foliage,
slackness blowing in the wind,
whipping empty air.

Loss exposes inner space
for unknown something new,
but only after long homesickness
for what will not return.
The willow chooses water
in which to sink its roots.

Tamarack's Widow

Had we been given
the gift of Ovid's
Baucis and Philemon
to grow old together
as trees,
what species, beloved,
would you have been?

Tall and exotic,
I imagine you the larch
which stood sentinel
before our home.
I'd never known one.
It was mysterious,
fragile, and precious,

and a paradox. Strong
source of posts, poles,
and railroad ties,
larch is a conifer
that rains needles
like sleet in winter.
You were like that.

But the gods
did not gift us
with long life.
Too soon, you
were dust and ashes.
Empty limbed, I dare
not dream of trees.

Anniversary Aubade

When we married you
sent an announcement
that called me poet.
But I think you feared her,
feared what she might see,
that she would say it.
And she did see,
but loved too much
to say anything.

I loved you, and
the poet in me dried up.
Now that you are gone,
the muse has returned.
In night's stillness
I pray and ponder,
write and wonder.
Now that my bed is empty,
my head is full of words.

But I would sweep
them all away to lie
in your arms again,
silent as the rising sun.

Desire

It was the quality of light
on this Pennsylvania back road
that put me in mind of mornings
that first sweet summer together
when you would come wandering up
from early work in the garden.
Clean with the smell of sweat and soil,
you'd strip off your shirt. I would quit
my chores. Sitting on the back porch
away from the world's prying eyes,
we'd listen to the creek, or laugh
gently at the ephemera
that makes a marriage bond and hold.
Though you are long since harvested,
and I at best am autumnal,
remembering makes me want you
as I did that shining summer.

That Fierce Space

On the topographical map
of human existence
pain is its own geography,
with Nepalese heights,
Dead Sea depths,
and deserts that
make believers
because they hide,
however meager, oases.

Plateaus follow,
calm after great suffering,
the quiet confidence
of having survived,
of having learned,
when reduced to nothing
but the fierce space
the body encompasses
it is enough.

Widow's *Déjà Vu*

Early this week, a hawk,
sharp eyed enough to see
small, succulent creatures
but not disaster,
crashed into the window.
It fluttered a bit
on the unfamiliar ground,
died with a puzzled look
in its wild, golden eye.

Yesterday, a second hawk,
solitary and splendid,
stood sentinel on the larch
above my murderous home.
Heloise in search of Abelard?
Aida keeping vigil?
No matter. I remembered,
and my heart fluttered
like a dying bird.

Fire into Life

It never broke
single digits today.
I fed a fire logs
of locust and cherry,
hot and aromatic.
I remembered
our first winter
in the old house
with no heat upstairs
but from grates
cut in the floor,
how in our small room
we discovered delicious
ways of warming
a cold season,
so much better
than last night's
bed socks,
extra blankets.
And I thought
this solitary morning
as I swept back ash,
unsmoored coals,
blew fire into life,
there are greater mysteries
in winter's shivering dark
than even the mystery
of flesh upon flesh.

Greek Lyric

Forty years ago,
hand in hand,
in the late afternoon
we climbed a mountain
on a Greek island
not knowing where we went.
It was an arid place,
stark and beautiful.

On the barren summit,
we sat silently.
The Aegean unfurled before us,
a bolt of azure velvet
absolutely still, untouched.
I was Penelope
watching for Odysseus
who was beside me.

The sun made for the horizon.
But before it rumpled
the sea's blue fabric,
the silver gray heavens opened.
One great shaft of light
moved across the water
toward the ragged coast of Delos---
and was gone.

Night came swiftly.
I am a solitary old woman now
who would not believe what they say,
that darkness is not dark to God,
that the night is as bright as the day,
save that I knew a hill in Greece,
remember a shaft of light,
and Aphrodite rising from the sea.

Lightning Source UK Ltd.
Milton Keynes UK
UKHW010707090222
398388UK00001B/74